I0435071

 U. S. Fish & Wildlife Service

Maine Wetlands and Waters:
Results of the National Wetlands Inventory

Maine Wetlands and Waters:
Results of the National Wetlands Inventory

June 2007

This page is intentionally blank.

Maine Wetlands and Waters:
Results of the National Wetlands Inventory

Ralph W. Tiner
U.S. Fish & Wildlife Service
National Wetlands Inventory Program
Northeast Region
300 Westgate Center Drive
Hadley, MA 01035

June 2007

This report should be cited as: Tiner, R.W. 2007. Maine Wetlands and Waters: Results of the National Wetlands Inventory. U.S. Fish and Wildlife Service, Northeast Region, Hadley, MA. NWI Technical Report. 22 pp.

Note: The findings and conclusions in the report are those of the author and do not necessarily represent the views of the U.S. Fish and Wildlife Service.

TABLE OF CONTENTS

Page

Introduction   1
    Study Area   1

Methods   4

Results   8
    Wetland Maps   8
    State Totals   10
    County Totals   10

Discussion   18
    Map Accuracy Assessment   18
    Comparison with Hydric Soils Acreage   18

Conclusion   20

Acknowledgments   21

References   22

This page is intentionally blank.

INTRODUCTION

The U.S. Fish and Wildlife Service (FWS) has been conducting a nationwide survey of wetlands and deepwater habitats since the mid-1970s through its National Wetlands Inventory Program (NWI). This survey is accomplished using traditional photointerpretation techniques to produces map and digital geospatial data on the status of wetlands. The U.S. Geological Survey topographic maps serve as the base data upon which boundaries of wetlands and deepwater habitats are delineated. Wetlands are classified according to the FWS's official wetland classification system (Cowardin et al. 1979) which has been adopted as the national standard for reporting on the status and trends of U.S. wetlands by the Federal Geographic Data Committee (http://www.fws.gov/stand/standards/wetlands.txt). Wetland mapping has been completed for over 90% of the coterminous U.S., all of Hawaii, and 35% of Alaska. For the Northeast, wetland mapping has been completed for 12 of the 13 states in the region; all but New York have been completely mapped. As time permits, the FWS summarizes the results of its NWI for geographic areas. Detailed state reports have been prepared for several states (Connecticut, Delaware, Maryland, and New Jersey), while data summary reports have been prepared for several other states in the northeastern U.S.: Massachusetts, Vermont, Pennsylvania, and West Virginia.

Wetland mapping for Maine was completed several years ago. Updated mapping is being done for the coastal region. This report provides a summary of the findings of the previous work.

Study Area

The state of Maine encompasses over 35,000 square miles in the northeastern United States. It ranks 39th among states in size and 40th in population. The state contains 30,862 square miles of land and 4,523 square miles of water (http://infoplease.com). From a natural landscape standpoint, the state falls within three of Bailey's ecoregions: Adirondack-New England Mixed Forest-Coniferous Forest-Alpine Meadow Province, Eastern Broadleaf Forest (Oceanic) Province, and Laurentian Mixed Forest Province (Bailey 1995). Due to its glacial history, the state contains thousands of lakes and ponds with Moosehead Lake and Sebago Lake being the most well-known. Among the more prominent rivers are the Penobscot, Kennebec, Androscoggin, Saco, St. John, Allagash, St. Croix (forming part of the state's eastern border with Canada), and Piscataqua (separating the state from New Hampshire). Maine's coastal region in noted for its irregular rocky shoreline which is 4,568 miles long or 7,039 miles long if the shorelines of its 4,617 islands are included in the calculation (Conkling 1999). Politically, the state is divided into 16 counties (Figure 1, Table 1).

Figure 1. Maine counties.

Table 1. Maine counties and their land and water area in square miles.
(http://en.wikipedia.org)

County	Land Area (% of total)	Water Area (% of total)	Total Area in Square Miles
Androscoggin	470 (94.6)	27 (5.4)	497
Aroostook	6,672 (97.7)	157 (2.3)	6,829
Cumberland	836 (68.7)	381 (31.3)	1,217
Franklin	1,698 (97.4)	46 (2.6)	1,744
Hancock	1,588 (67.5)	763 (32.5)	2,351
Kennebec	868 (91.2)	84 (8.8)	952
Knox	366 (32.0)	776 (68.0)	1,142
Lincoln	456 (65.1)	244 (34.9)	700
Oxford	2,078 (95.5)	97 (4.5)	2,175
Penobscot	3,396 (95.5)	160 (4.5)	3,556
Piscataquis	3,966 (90.6)	411 (9.4)	4,377
Sagadahoc	254 (68.6)	116 (31.4)	370
Somerset	3,926 (95.9)	169 (4.1)	4,095
Washington	2,569 (78.9)	686 (21.1)	3,255
Waldo	730 (85.6)	123 (14.4)	853
York	991 (78.0)	280 (22.0)	1,271
Total	30,864 (87.2)	4,520 (12.8)	35,384

METHODS

The NWI relies on photointerpretation of aerial photographs to locate and map wetlands and deepwater habitats. For Maine, most of the aerial photography used was 1:58,000 color infrared captured in the spring of 1985 and 1986, with some photos acquired in 1983 and 1984. With this imagery, the target mapping unit for wetlands ranges between 1-3 acres. This means that most wetlands larger than three acres should be mapped and that all wetlands are not mapped. Even with this target mapping unit established, it must be recognized that aerial photointerpretation has limitations in terms of the types of wetlands that can be readily identified (Tiner 1990, 1999) and that larger wetlands of certain types will escape detection and be missing from the maps. These limitations are generally outlined in Table 1, with other observations from recent updated mapping listed in Table 2.

Wetlands were classified according to the FWS's official wetland classification system (Cowardin et al. 1979). The following categories were identified for wetlands and deepwater habitats: system, subsystem, class, subclass, water regime, and a few special modifiers (e.g., partly drained, dike/impounded, excavated, and farmed). The organic soil modifier "g" was applied to Atlantic white cedar swamps (e.g., PFO4Bg) to highlight them; the acid modifier "a" was applied to bogs (e.g., PSS3Ba). The "h" (impounded) modifier was applied to many wetlands fragmented by roads as well as to diked wetlands.

Wetland maps were prepared following standard NWI mapping conventions (U.S. Fish and Wildlife Service 1994, 1995). Data were digitized to create a geospatial database. NWI data are posted on the web at NWI home page: http://www.fws.gov/nwi/. Data were summarized by the NWI Mapping Support Center at Madison, Wisconsin. The following conventions were employed:

- State and county boundaries were determined using the Geographic Data Technology's 1:100K states and counties layers. These were used due to the lack of a consistent nationwide layer of boundaries at the 1:24,000 scale.
- All marine deepwater habitats (M1___) were removed from the analysis. The decision to remove them from the analysis was made due to the lack of validity of this acreage value. The marine system extends far beyond the mapped area and is ended at 1:250K quad boundaries rendering the acreage meaningless.
- Areas where county or state boundaries consisted of two-line waterbodies, (i.e. rivers, streams) the boundary was identified and digitized directly from a USGS 1:24,000 DRG.

The data was summarized by county and aggregated by state in two categories: 1) system, subsystem, class, and subclass and 2) system and water regime. Any differences in state and county totals are due to round-off procedures.

Table 1. Major NWI map limitations. (Adapted from Tiner 1999).

1. Target mapping unit – minimum size wetland that NWI is attempting to map which is generally related to the scale of the imagery: 1-3 acres for 1:58,000 photography used in the study area.

2. Spring photography – aquatic beds and nonpersistent emergent wetlands may be undermapped since these types are usually obscured by high water. In some cases, flooded emergents may be misclassified as scrub-shrub wetlands.

3. Forested wetlands – forested wetlands on glacial till are difficult to photointerpret as are temporarily flooded or seasonally saturated types, especially on the coastal plain and on glaciolacustrine plains; they may be underrepresented by the current NWI mapping. Such areas may be identified by examining U.S. Department of Agriculture soil survey maps for hydric soil map units that are undeveloped (i.e., areas of undeveloped hydric soil map units that were not mapped by NWI represent areas that may contain wetlands).

4. Estuarine and tidal waters – delineation of the break between estuarine and riverine (tidal) systems should be considered approximate; the irregular rocky shore of the coast of Maine has complicated the delineation of the boundary between estuarine and marine systems and such boundaries are also approximate.

5. Tidal flats – since imagery was not tide synchronized, tidal flat boundaries were based on aerial photointerpretation in consultation with collateral data such as U.S. Geological Survey topographic maps and Maine coastal geologic maps (Timson 1976).

6. Coastal wetlands – identification of high marsh (irregularly flooded) vs. low marsh (regularly flooded) in tidal marshes is conservative; photo-signatures are not distinctive in many instances.

7. Water regimes – water regime classification is based on photo-signatures coupled with limited field verification; they should be considered approximate.

8. Linear wetlands (long, narrow) – they follow drainageways and stream corridors and may or may not be mapped depending on project objectives. Most NWI maps identify at least some of these features, but no attempt was made to map all of them.

9. Partly drained wetlands – they are conservatively mapped; many are not shown on NWI maps.

10. Aerial photography – imagery reflects wetness during the specific year and season it was acquired. Some photos for northern Maine were very dark making it difficult to detect forested wetlands.

11. Drier-end wetlands (temporarily flooded and seasonally saturated types) – they are difficult to photointerpret; many have been mapped by consulting hydric soil data from the U.S.D.A. Natural Resources Conservation Service.

12. Mapped boundaries – they may be somewhat different than if based on detailed field observations, especially in areas with subtle changes in topography.

Table 2. Some recent observations regarding limitations of prior Maine NWI mapping for Downeast Maine (Huber 2006). These changes will be made to the updated NWI maps; they were not made to the data referenced in this report.

1. Many wetlands mapped as PFO1 (palustrine broad-leaved deciduous forested wetland) are actually dominated by larch (Larix laricina) and should be classified as PFO2 (2 = needle-leaved deciduous).

2. Numerous smaller wetlands that occur in dips between rolling hills were not mapped.

3. Areas mapped as M2AB1N (algae-dominated rocky shores) appear to have less algae than before and are better classified as M2RS1N and M2RS2N or mixes.

4. Significant tidal flow was observed through culverts connecting wetlands upstream with marine wetlands downstream and many wetlands previously classified as palustrine tidal wetlands should be reclassified as marine or estuarine types.

RESULTS

Wetland Maps

NWI maps for Maine were prepared for various location from the late 1970s to the present. These maps were produced at a scale of 1:24,000 using the U.S. Geological Survey topographic maps as base maps. Hardcopy maps are available for purchase through the Maine Geological Survey (Publications), Augusta, ME 04333-0033 (Robert Tucker, 207-287-2801).

After publication of the hardcopy maps, the NWI maps were converted to digital form for computer access and geographic information system (GIS) applications. Since the 1990s, the NWI Program has stopped production of hardcopy maps, replacing them with digital wetland geospatial data. All NWI data are now available online at the NWI website: http://www.fws.gov/nwi/. While the entire state was mapped by the late 1980s, some areas (coastal region – New Hampshire border to Machias) have been updated with more recent imagery. These newer data are only available online. To access NWI data, visit the NWI website, click on the "Wetlands Mapper", then click on the map of the lower 48 states, and finally zoom into the location of interest to see the wetland data for a specific area. Digital NWI data can also be downloaded for GIS use at this website.

Figure 2 shows the distribution of wetlands and waters of Maine, excluding marine waters. This figure is a reduction of the original map that was prepared at a scale of 1:450,000.

8

Figure 2. Map showing the distribution of wetlands and waters of Maine excluding waters of coastal embayments and the Gulf of Maine. (Note: This is a reduced version of original figure.)

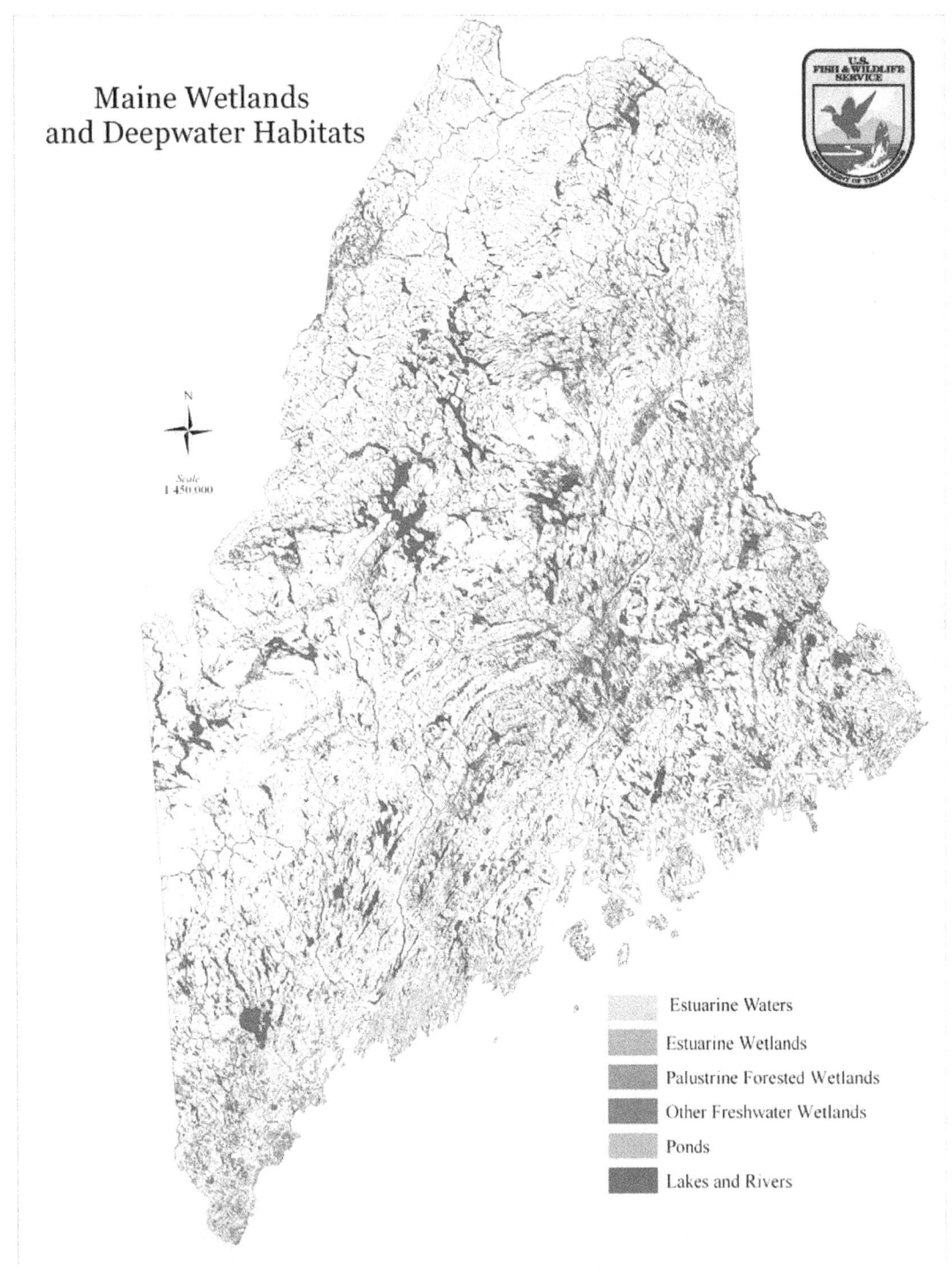

State Totals

Wetlands. The NWI identified more than two million acres of wetlands, covering 10.3% of the state's land area (Table 3). Palustrine wetlands are the main type, totaling 1.9 million acres and representing 94% of the state's wetland area. Fifty-nine percent of the palustrine wetlands (or 56% of all wetlands) were forested types, with scrub-shrub wetlands making up slightly more than one-quarter (28%) of the freshwater wetlands, emergent wetlands representing 9% of these wetlands, and ponds (unconsolidated bottom and shores) account for nearly 3%. Estuarine wetlands are second-ranked in area, occupying roughly 69,000 acres which amount to slightly more than 3% of the wetland area. Tidal flats (unconsolidated shores) were the most common estuarine wetlands, accounting for 62% of the estuarine wetlands. Emergent wetlands (salt and brackish marshes) made up 28% of the estuarine wetlands. Marine wetlands represented 2% of the state's wetlands. Rocky shores (including aquatic beds which are mostly algae-covered rocky shores) accounted for 55% of these wetlands, while tidal flats (unconsolidated shores) comprised nearly all of the remainder.

Deepwater Habitats. Over one million acres of deepwater habitats were inventoried, excluding marine waters and waters of linear streams. Lacustrine waters accounted for 86% of the state's water area (912,282 acres). Riverine waters were next in area with 87,293 acres mapped (6,722 tidal acres, 65,041 lower perennial acres, and 15,530 upper perennial acres), followed by 53,491 acres of estuarine waters (including 11 acres of eelgrass beds). It must be recognized, however, that marine waters dominate the state's waters but were not tabulated.

County Totals

Wetlands. The acreage of wetlands by type is given for each county in Table 4. Aroostook County had the most wetland acreage with nearly 430,000 acres inventoried. Five counties had over 200,000 acres: Aroostook, Penobscot, Washington, Piscataquis, and Somerset. The wetlands in these counties accounted for 70% of the state wetlands (the counties represent 67% of the state's land area). The highest density of wetlands was found in Sagadahoc County with nearly 21% of its land area occupied by wetlands (Table 5). Eight other counties had more than 10% of their land area represented by wetlands.

Deepwater Habitats. When marine waters are excluded, Piscataquis County had the highest acreage of deepwater habitat (Table 6). This acreage was almost twice that of the second-ranked county – Washington, which had nearly 130,000 acres of these waterbodies. Nine percent of Piscataquis County was represented by water; this was the highest percentage among counties. Kennebec closely followed with 8.7% of the county being water, but this was attributed to only 53,000 acres of waterbodies. If marine waters are counted, Knox County becomes top-ranked, closely followed by Hancock County (Table 7). Washington County is the only other county with more than 500 square miles of water. Penobscot County dropped to ninth place in the ranking when marine waters were included in the calculation.

Table 3. Wetland acreage summaries for the state of Maine. State totals differ from sum of county totals due to round-off procedures. (Note: Marine and estuarine aquatic beds are nearly all algae-covered rocky shores.)

Ecological System	Wetland Class	Acreage
Marine	Aquatic Bed	18,950
	Reef	15
	Rocky Shore	3,200
	Unconsolidated Shore	18,217
	------------------------------	------
	Subtotal Nonvegetated	21,432
	Total Marine	*40,382*
Estuarine	Aquatic Bed	6,641
	Emergent	19,653
	Scrub-Shrub	9
	------------------------------	----------
	Subtotal Vegetated	26,303
	Rocky Shore	607
	Unconsolidated Shore	42,933
	------------------------------	----------
	Subtotal Nonvegetated	43,540
	Total Estuarine	*69,843*
Palustrine	Aquatic Bed	220
	Emergent	179,496
	Forested	1,133,591
	Scrub-Shrub	541,108
	------------------------------	-------------
	Subtotal Vegetated	1,854,415
	Unconsolidated Bottom	53,737
	Unconsolidated Shore	736
	------------------------------	-------------
	Subtotal Nonvegetated	54,473
	Total Palustrine	*1,908,888*

Table 3 (continued).

Lacustrine	Aquatic Bed	94
	Emergent (nonpersistent)	31
	----------------------------------	-------------
	Subtotal Vegetated	125
	Rocky Shore	7,948
	Unconsolidated Bottom	188
	Unconsolidated Shore	7,446
	----------------------------------	-------------
	Subtotal Nonvegetated	15,582
	Total Lacustrine	*15,707*
Riverine	Aquatic Bed (tidal)	10
	Rocky Shore (tidal)	4
	Unconsolidated Shore (tidal)	475
	Unconsolidated Shore	2,236
	Rocky Shore	42
	----------------------------------	-----------
	Total Riverine	*2,767*
ALL WETLANDS		**2,037,587**

Table 4. NWI findings for each county. Numbers represent acres of wetlands.

County

NWI Type	Androscoggin	Aroostook	Cumberland	Franklin	Hancock	Kennebec	Knox	Lincoln
Palustrine Wetlands								
Aquatic Bed	--	28	8	23	53	3	4	--
Emergent	2,874	24,517	3,862	5,092	11,695	7,911	2,343	5,332
Forested	15,227	303,000	20,856	27,196	48,735	24,999	9,616	18,691
Scrub-Shrub	5,850	90,739	9,323	15,837	33,870	14,923	4,638	8,513
Unconsol. Bottom	810	9,622	2,054	2,654	3,253	1,505	862	1,141
Lacustrine Wetlands								
Aquatic Bed	--	--	--	--	70	--	13	--
Unconsol. Shore	87	94	13	1	--	25	--	--
Rocky Shore	1	--	--	--	1	--	--	--
Riverine Wetlands								
Unconsol. Shore	--	1,065	2	309	--	125	12	128
Rocky Shore	25	3	--	--	--	1	--	1
Estuarine Wetlands								
Aquatic Bed	--	--	61	--	2,565	--	485	889
Emergent	--	--	4,034	--	1,015	--	504	1,309
Unconsol. Shore	--	--	5,238	--	8,675	--	3,228	5,161
Rocky Shore	--	--	10	--	321	--	21	89
Marine Wetlands								
Aquatic Bed	--	--	787	--	7,687	--	2,880	553
Unconsol. Shore	--	--	2,441	--	3,164	--	1,652	162
Rocky Shore	--	--	163	--	1,446	--	416	118
Reef	--	--	--	--	15	--	--	--
Total	24,874	429,068	48,852	51,112	122,565	49,492	26,674	42,087

Table 4 (continued).

County

NWI Type	Oxford	Penobscot	Piscataquis	Sagadahoc	Somerset	Washington	Waldo	York
Palustrine Wetlands								
Aquatic Bed	1	7	--	39	33	1	3	15
Emergent	6,114	29,671	21,007	2,636	20,724	24,335	5,395	5,990
Forested	39,322	176,750	140,031	17,384	113,951	106,323	23,289	48,221
Scrub-Shrub	21,513	100,163	67,714	2,127	57,598	79,811	13,840	14,649
Unconsol. Bottom	2,699	6,976	6,543	555	5,908	5,182	1,652	3,059
Lacustrine Wetlands								
Aquatic Bed	--	--	--	--	--	--	--	11
Emergent	31	--	--	--	--	--	--	--
Unconsol. Shore	18	5	3,829	--	3,162	209	--	3
Unconsol. Bottom	29	--	1	--	5	139	--	14
Rocky Shore	--	531	6,295	--	937	184	--	--
Riverine Wetlands								
Unconsol. Shore	234	261	138	43	255	155	7	1
Rocky Shore	--	4	7	--	3	--	--	--
Estuarine Wetlands								
Aquatic Bed	--	--	--	143	--	2,233	184	81
Emergent	--	4	--	4,814	--	3,471	422	4,089
Unconsol. Shore	--	180	--	4,886	--	11,882	718	2,965
Rocky Shore	--	--	--	49	--	73	44	2
Marine Wetlands								
Aquatic Bed	--	--	--	84	--	4,463	1,827	669
Unconsol. Shore	--	--	--	578	--	7,953	707	1,560
Rocky Shore	--	--	--	88	--	833	103	35
Total	69,961	314,552	245,565	33,426	202,576	247,247	48,191	81,364

14

Table 5. Ranking of counties by wetland area. Percent of county comprised by wetlands is also given.

Rank	County	Wetland Acreage	Percent of County Land Area
1	Aroostook	429,068	10.0
2	Penobscot	314,552	14.5
3	Washington	247,247	15.0
4	Piscataquis	245,565	9.7
5	Somerset	202,576	8.1
6	Hancock	122,565	12.1
7	York	81,364	12.8
8	Oxford	69,961	5.3
9	Franklin	51,112	4.7
10	Kennebec	49,492	8.9
11	Cumberland	48,852	9.1
12	Waldo	48,191	10.3
13	Lincoln	42,087	14.4
14	Sagadahoc	33,426	20.6
15	Knox	26,674	11.4
16	Androscoggin	24,874	8.3

Table 6. Acreage of deepwater habitats in Maine counties. Riverine waters are separated into lower perennial, upper perennial, and tidal types. Percent of county occupied by deepwater habitats (both excluding and including marine waters) is given.

County	Lacustrine Waters	Riverine Waters			Estuarine Waters	Total Waters	% of County (% w/Marine*)
		Lower	Upper	Tidal			
Androscoggin	13,041	3,746	--	--	--	16,787	5.3 (5.3)
Aroostook	78,724	14,789	6,758	--	--	100,271	2.3 (2.3)
Cumberland	51,001	1,571	12	438	8,329	61,351	7.8 (31.3)
Franklin	28,838	1,479	436	--	--	30,752	(2.8) (2.8)
Hancock	64,756	995	153	5	12,643	78,552	5.2 (32.5)
Kennebec	48,107	3,725	5	1,435	13	53,285	8.7 (8.8)
Knox	6,777	157	6	84	3,608	10,632	1.5 (68.0)
Lincoln	11,462	389	113	1,023	8,384	21,371	4.8 (34.9)
Oxford	56,395	5,311	338	--	--	62,044	4.5 (4.5)
Penobscot	80,888	14,356	2,910	635	564	99,353	4.3 (4.5)
Piscataquis	245,315	5,283	1,717	--	--	252,315	9.0 (9.0)
Sagadahoc	1,018	116	--	2,958	2,958	7,050	3.0 (31.4)
Somerset	87,193	6,611	1,490	--	--	95,294	3.6 (3.6)
Washington	113,557	3,406	1,445	143	10,913	129,464	6.2 (21.1)
Waldo	12,578	809	146	--	2,731	16,264	3.0 (14.4)
York	10,630	2,300	1	--	3,347	16,278	2.0 (22.0)

*Estimated.

Table 7. Ranking of counties by deepwater habitat area. Area is square miles.

County	Nontidal Waters	Tidal Waters*	Total Waters	Rank
Androscoggin	26.2	--	26.2	16
Aroostook	156.7	--	156.7	10
Cumberland	82.2	298.8	381.0	5
Franklin	48.1	--	48.1	15
Hancock	103.0	660.0	763.0	2
Kennebec	81.0	3.0	84.0	14
Knox	10.8	765.2	776.0	1
Lincoln	18.7	225.3	244.0	7
Oxford	97.0	--	97.0	13
Penobscot	153.4	6.6	160.0	9
Piscataquis	394.2	--	394.2	4
Sagadahoc	1.8	114.2	116.0	12
Somerset	148.9	--	148.9	8
Washington	185.0	501.0	686.0	3
Waldo	21.1	101.9	123.0	11
York	20.2	259.8	280.0	6

*Area of marine waters was estimated.

DISCUSSION

Map Accuracy Assessment

A map accuracy investigation was performed for the area under jurisdiction of the Maine Land Use Regulation Commission (LURC) in 1994 (Nichols 1994). The study involved examining 1740 points along 90 transects in northwestern, northern, and eastern Maine. All areas designated by NWI as wetlands or deepwater habitats were mapped correctly as one or the other resource type. NWI maps identified over 90% of the wetlands greater than 3 acres in size along the sample transects. For areas mapped as upland, 93-97% of such areas were actually upland, with the rest largely being unmapped wetlands. The total percent of sample points that were correctly mapped to resource type was 95.4%. Some wetlands were included as uplands due to mapping conventions (e.g., minimum mapping units) or misidentification. For areas mapped as wetlands, cover type classification was correct for over 90% of the points examined, with most of the discrepancies attributed to changes (e.g., beaver activity and human-induced impacts) since the date of the aerial photographs used for the mapping.

If 7% of the area designated by NWI as upland is considered wetland, 1.24 million acres should be added to the NWI wetland acreage for Maine. This would give Maine a total of 3.28 million acres of wetlands, occupying an estimated 16.7% of the state.

Comparison with Hydric Soil Acreage

The U.S.D.A. National Resources Conservation Service has provided hydric soil acreage summaries for surveyed areas in Maine which represent about 75% of the state (Table 8). Hydric soils may cover 19% of the state, while the NWI mapping identified only 10% of the state as wetland or nearly 17% if wetlands predicted on NWI uplands (based on the Nichols study) are added to the mapped NWI wetlands. The difference is likely due to both limitations of wetland photointerpretation and wetland alterations. Photointerpretation has problems detecting certain evergreen forested wetlands in an evergreen forest landscape matrix and identifying drier-end wetlands (those on soils with seasonal high water tables, but not subject to flooding). The soil survey data also include former wetlands such as drained hydric soils or hydric soils that are now developed (e.g., filled for commercial, industrial, or residential property). Overall, the NWI mapping is conservative, while the hydric soil estimates are more liberal and don't reflect recent wetland losses (i.e., conversion of hydric soils to nonwetlands), so Maine's current wetland acreage may encompass about 17% of the state.

Table 8. Hydric soil data for Maine. Percent of survey area predicted to be covered by hydric soil is also given. (Source: USDA Natural Resources Conservation Service)

County Area Surveyed (Acres)	Acreage of Hydric Soils	% of Survey Area
Cumberland and part of Oxford (689,331)	82,765	12.0
Kennebec (609,197)	98,077	16.1
Waldo (492,723)	84,323	17.0
York (656,844)	158,529	24.1
Knox and Lincoln (654,701)	98,790	15.1
Somerset-Southern Part (691,174)	185,994	26.9
Androscoggin and Sagadahoc (512,275)	70,993	13.9
Aroostook – Northeast (1,554,443)	374,351	24.0
Aroostook – South (1,006,646)	320,175	31.8
Franklin and part of Somerset (773,146)	94,916	12.3
Oxford (934,873)	86,825	9.3
Hancock (881,668)	123,202	14.0
Penobscot (1,501,216)	403,119	26.9
Piscataquis – South (687,000)	140,043	20.4
Washington (1,129,038)	225,911	20.0
Somerset and parts of Franklin and Oxford (2,114,821)	289,911	13.7
Total Survey Area (14,889,206)	2,837,144	19.1

CONCLUSION

The NWI Program mapped about 2.04 million acres of wetlands and over 1 million acres of deepwater habitats, excluding marine waters. The wetland mapping is conservative due to limitations of the photointerpretation techniques employed. Considering NRCS hydric soil data and the results of a wetland map assessment done for the LURC region, the actual extent of wetlands in Maine is likely somewhere between 3.28 and 3.75 million acres, representing 17-19% of the state's land area.

ACKNOWLEDGMENTS

Numerous individuals contributed to the mapping of Maine's wetlands. The Maine Land Use Regulatory Commission (LURC) provided funding to inventory the lands under their jurisdiction. Fred Todd (LURC) was instrumental in getting this area of the state mapped by the NWI. The U.S.D.A. Natural Resources Conservation Service provided some funding for work in the southwestern part of the state. Bob Wengynck assisted with this support. Ralph Tiner coordinated this inventory for the U.S. Fish and Wildlife Service (FWS).

Wetland photointerpretation for the mid-1980s survey was performed by staff at Geonex-Martel Inc. (St. Petersburg, FL) including Joanne Weber, Charles Messenkopf, Tom Kunneke, L. Cornell, and Toni Alese. The coastal areas and neighboring inland regions were originally photointerpreted by the University of Massachusetts, Forestry and Wildlife Department by John Organ, Frank Shumway, Tim Moore, and Anthony Davis, with a few areas done by Jonathan Hall (Martel Laboratories). These late 1970s data were updated.

Field review of draft maps was done by summer assistants including Susan Ziegler, E. Davis, Bob Houston, Chris Hamilton, Chris Nichols, Matt Burne, and Irene Huber. FWS personnel assisting in field review included Wende (Rosier) Mahaney, Gordon Russell, Porter Reed, Norm Mangrum, Maurry Mills, Rene Whitehead, Glenn Smith, and Ralph Tiner. Chris Nichols conducted an accuracy assessment of the maps which was funded by LURC.

Glenn Smith (FWS) was responsible for providing regional quality control of the inventory products, while Norm Mangrum and Rene Whitehead (FWS) provided national quality control. Cartographic work was performed under the direction of the FWS's National Wetlands Inventory Center, St. Petersburg, Florida. GIS analysis of the data for this report was done by Mitch Bergeson (U.S. Geological Survey) working for the NWI Mapping Support Center at Madison, Wisconsin.

Paul R. Finnell, USDA Natural Resources Conservation Service, National Soil Survey Center, Lincoln, Nebraska provided summaries of hydric soil data for Maine used to prepare Table 9.

REFERENCES

Bailey, R.G. 1995. Description of the Ecoregions of the United States. U.S.D.A. Forest Service, Washington, DC. http://www.fs.fed.us/land/ecosysmgmt/ecoreg1_home.html

Conkling, P.W. 1999. Islands in Time: A Natural and Cultural History of the Islands of the Gulf of Maine. Island Institute, Rockland, ME.

Cowardin, L.M., V. Carter, F.C. Golet, and E.T. LaRoe. 1979. Classification of Wetlands and Deepwater Habitats of the United States. U.S. Fish and Wildlife Service, Washington, DC. FWS/OBS-79/31.

Huber, I. 2006. Field trip summary report for coastal Maine tier 2. University of Massachusetts, Natural Resources Group, Amherst, MA.

Nichols, C. 1994. Map Accuracy of National Wetlands Inventory Maps for Areas Subject to Land Use Regulation Commission Jurisdiction. U.S. Fish and Wildlife Service, Hadley, MA. Ecological Services report R5-94/6.

Timson, B.S. 1976. Coastal marine geologic environment maps. Maine Geological Survey. Open-file maps. 76-121.

Tiner, R.W., Jr. 1990. Use of high-altitude aerial photography for inventorying forested wetlands in the United States. For. Ecol. Manage. 33/34: 593-604.

Tiner, R.W. 1999. Wetland Indicators: A Guide to Wetland Identification, Delineation, Classification, and Mapping. Lewis Publishers, CRC Press, Boca Raton, FL.

U.S. Fish and Wildlife Service. 1995. Photo Interpretation Conventions for the National Wetlands Inventory. NWI Project, St. Petersburg, FL.

U.S. Fish and Wildlife Service. 1994. Cartographic Conventions for the National Wetlands Inventory. NWI Project, St. Petersburg, FL.

This page is intentionally blank.

U.S. Department of the Interior
Fish and Wildlife Service

http://www.fws.gov

June 2007